I SLEEP IN THE ARMS
OF YOUR EYES

ESSENTIAL POETS SERIES 251

**Canada Council Conseil des Arts
for the Arts   du Canada**

**ONTARIO ARTS COUNCIL
CONSEIL DES ARTS DE L'ONTARIO**

an Ontario government agency
un organisme du gouvernement de l'Ont

Canada

Guernica Editions Inc. acknowledges the support of the Canada Council
for the Arts and the Ontario Arts Council. The Ontario Arts Council
is an agency of the Government of Ontario.

We acknowledge the financial support of the Government of Canada.

BEVERLY ELLENBOGEN

I SLEEP IN THE ARMS OF YOUR EYES

GUERNICA
EDITIONS

TORONTO – BUFFALO – LANCASTER (U.K.)
2018

Michael Mirolla, general editor
Elana Wolff, editor
Cover and interior design: Errol F. Richardson
Guernica Editions Inc.
1569 Heritage Way, Oakville, (ON), Canada L6M 2Z7
2250 Military Road, Tonawanda, N.Y. 14150-6000 U.S.A.
www.guernicaeditions.com

Distributors:
University of Toronto Press Distribution,
5201 Dufferin Street, Toronto (ON), Canada M3H 5T8
Gazelle Book Services, White Cross Mills
High Town, Lancaster LA1 4XS U.K.

First edition.
Printed in Canada.

Legal Deposit – Third Quarter
Library of Congress Catalog Card Number: 2017964545
Library and Archives Canada Cataloguing in Publication
Ellenbogen, Beverly, author
I sleep in the arms of your eyes / Beverly Ellenbogen. -- First edition.

(Essential poets series ; 251)
Poems.
ISBN 978-1-77183-246-5 (softcover)

I. Title. II. Series: Essential poets ; 251

PS8609.L538I88 2018   C811'.6   C2018-900148-8

For Shaul

Contents

A Path Once Light

Yesterday
I walked the trail
we walked,
the snow was
heavier though.

This winter weaves
from day to day.
A path once
light in frozen air
is thick with rain again.

I walked the path
we walked
and found the place
you pushed me down
in play,

I found the place I fell
off the end of my question
into your answer,

I showed you where I spent
my solitude
and all the words I shared
were still and fallen there.

Shift

I once worked the day shift
in a graveyard. In the speckled dawn
I stabbed my trowel
into the shaded beds

that stretched before each stone.
Filled rainbow arcs and patterned
weaves, sunny waves
like bibs on granite necks.

I learned the names of
tastefully tight blooms and
resilient borders: dusty miller,
geranium, salvia, alyssum.

Whenever I walk
through the parks and city grounds
I can still list them
in my head.

Back then we hunted grape leaves
during our lunch break,
found those that
grew beneath the willows,

dipping into the green corners
from neighbouring yards.
We brought our harvest
to parents' homes,

filled them with rice and garlic.
Playing domestic, with
summer jobs and cars
on loan from empty-nester parents

not at home. Summer after
my first year at university,
the path ahead not visible
beyond the rows of flowers.

Beneath Our Feet

I have been left a late friend's
IQ test kit. Adult Intelligence Scale.
You can see he never administered it.
Clean puzzles nest in cardboard creased with mould.

It's spring across the cemetery's face.
Like him, the season deceives.
Snow disassembles the warm air,
mud freezing to an awkward

grimace beneath our feet. A dark eye is shutting
over his body. Perhaps he realized
only a god-sized cipher would be
big enough to hide him. Our hearts

proved too small. The damp test box
is the colour of his thin fingers –
the tenacious, pale grip
of something unmeasurable.

March

This year spring
comes because

I stopped
waiting for it.

It comes dandying
with yellow lions,

waggling
seeds and

clover sprouts
that march

down the line
of patio stones.

So much,
too late.

Green amnesia,
weedy hubris.

Horse or No Horse

Dear Mummy and Daddy
I want to go home
this Sunday —

in an envelope marked "nostalgia"
this letter has survived my grandmother's
progressive purges
as she lightens herself
of our words:
Gone are decades
of camp letters,
birthday wishes,
holiday greetings.

She bends to read,
a thin shoulder of memory
rising and falling.

These days she has a new need
for our company,
much else remains the same:

the gentle brown skin rolling over her hips
as she shamelessly changes clothes,
on the move from one room to another,

the way she holds a spoon in conversation.

Dear Mummy and Daddy, she reads,

I want to go home this Sunday
because I'm not having a nice time here

Horse or no horse ... "

He loved horses, she interrupts to tell me,
so I sent him to a camp that had horses –

Dear Mummy and Daddy,

I want to go home this Sunday
because I'm not having a nice time here.
Horse or no horse, I don't like this place.
So long for now.
Remember to send me a letter.
And please send my high boots and jeans.

She folds the fifty-two-year-old
piece of paper –

Is this from the *same* son
who told her the caregiver
would be staying overnight?
Someone has boldly put clothes
in *her* bedroom closet.

Horse or no horse –

she sits on the edge of the couch,
not always sure how to have a nice time
either.

Wandering toward the calendar,
she touches the pills,
thinks of calling someone
she may have just called,
agrees to a trip to the mall
where the salesladies call her by name.
Raising her chin,
she imperiously waves a hand
You see? They *all* know me!

But after her return
the feeling is lost
on the winding route
between the African violet
and knitted afghan,

between the window panes
that frame the cathedral light
as it flips over Mount Royal each night,

replaced now by a small smile
and sad eyes:

Horse or no horse, she breathes.

Exposure

I grew up in
this forest circuit,
went to camp here,
paddled the lake,
learned to love the water
dip and swing.

Hung upside down in a kayak
with nose-plugs and rubber
goggles,
watching the counselor's
legs as he waited,
waited for me to roll.

I wasn't going to roll.

I hung there upside down,
algae swirling in ribbons
of sunlight,
the counselor's blue-white
feet disappearing
in sand.

Hair – wet strings,
I made a pinhole camera
later and lurked
in the cattails,
held on still
for exposure.

By April

her own name
and phone
number
filled the margins

of the calendar
tacked up outside
the kitchen.
This, after months

where each day
was marked with
a thin,
shaky *X*,

transforming
pages into a
stuttering
treasure map;

the cache
of each day
lost
by nightfall.

So we walked her out
one morning,
on an outing,
then into

a new home.
A place
where calendars
held little power,

neither predictive
nor redemptive.
Each day is welcomed
as itself, no other.

But I find myself
even less able
to embrace
one moment at a time.
I roll myself up in the
linens I took from her
closet,
inhale memory:

that path
of our breath
through fabric,
that print

of her feet on mine,
dark mornings
when she slept in
our basement

and welcomed
thin arms, our
cold soles
beneath the covers.

Birds Found Today in Australia

were imported by a 19th century
English acclimatization committee

that followed a Shakespearean directive:
Transport two of each species

found in a sonnet. Thus
was the biodiversity of a continent

consumed. And so roam our efforts to
feel at home: somewhere between

the welcome ache of memory
and a longing for destruction.

Brought Back

Somewhere in the
knee deep wheat grass
of Emery the writing
soul of a man walks
with fingertips weaving
through beads of grain.

Then, the sky inverts,
wheat chaff blows upward,
and a tangle of sheets wad into a blue
sun between his knees, trail
under the empty bed:

Write about this,
buzzes in his head.

He, the poet who dreams
of prophetic farmers,
lives on the east coast
but is returning soon.

He,
whose blue eyes take in
with mild surprise
the steak he ordered
as it appears in a sushi roll

then mentions Blake
and Purdy and the movie
The Wedding Crashers
almost in one breath,
shoulders shaking
with held laughter.

He, who may be shy,
but is caught
by her and
brought back
just in time.

Runaway

You hold a runaway child
to your chest for fifty years
and he melts into your breath,
becomes your runaway soul.

I imagine such a soul
is hard on the heart;
furtive, always hungry,
curious, endlessly alone.

Sun glints off the windows,
violent sparks envelop cars
far below and
and faint calls of workmen

bound off concrete walls.
And your pen scratches,
scratches its beat,
beats your heart across the page.

You talk of boxes.
Never discarding a word,
boxes of paper hold you tight.
Imagine – they are boxes of hearts.

Old hearts. A documented
collection. Because, you ask,
what can I do when I am alone
but pretend I am not alone?

Shadows inch up the brick
walls and deep below this room
a subway throbs through
underground tunnels.

A runaway soul must use up
hearts quickly. Beauty turns
breathless, the sadness
of others is drowning.

In fact, just now, I saw you slip one heart into
your pocket and wind up a new one.
When you get home you will gently
lay the still heart in a box and write
the date and time and weather
on its lid: *May 21, 2009:*
unseasonably hot, spring day
Around the room are stacks of love

and memory. Packed in tissue, straw,
foam chips that click with static.
A legion of hearts to keep you company
as you follow your runaway soul,

writing a revisionary life.

Primary

Do you remember the woman
with the translucent children?
Remember her face,
smooth as the snow,
and her clear eyes,
beneath the flossy halo of
hair? The piping of her
voice, how it
made the other children
stare, and look at their boots?
The pale wandering eyes
of her daughter and her small
boy, their clothes of
primary colours, like toys:
blue boots, red jacket,
yellow hat. Remember
how she walked them home in
a fur coat round as
a bell tolling
to their march
every afternoon?
Well, I saw her again
this winter, at the
intersection near the
pizza place, and little had changed,
except for her brow –
not quite as clear.

Her son,
not quite as primary –
a certain tired look
to his chapped mouth,
hard set of his chin.

Furnished with Forgetting

My children thrive
from flower pots of the mind,

and what I can afford:

things given away,
content sales, thrift stores

furnished with forgetting
they come together,

difficult to tidy, always
on their way elsewhere.

Light Losing Ground

Cooking oil warms in an iron pan.
Can we go to the library?
When will it be dinner?
They fill blank sheets of paper
with rows of felt tipped hearts, the
same bright daisy eyes. Winter
packs its cold air against glass
and the kitchen becomes
a bunker, until spring
can thaw all those
marker smiles and lines of sky.
This is the window
where my heart tears
through, or stays behind.
This is how time passes,
children's shadows
cast upon the wooden floor.

Robes of Water

In a street
lamp's

stage-like
cast of light

through the
upstairs

hall, stands a
door

through which
I tread

in robes
of water.

Buoyed
beneath

an infant's
cry,

my feet
turn pages –

dreams
of psalms,

how much
more than me

I come to be.

Reach

Metaphors track me like butterflies on a migratory path, wing beats driving against my ears. When I pinch my son's thumb in his jacket zipper the creatures careen unbalanced across my mind: I bend down, reach my finger through one white, plastic-covered wire mesh square of his hockey mask to touch the tears on his cheeks as I lift him from behind, though I am only on my knees.

I am Asleep yet My Heart is Awake

A single slat of the blind is bent:
Each receives the next except for one,
where my son matches an eye to the black morning
glass. There is something beating. It is me,
watching his wakeful chest:
lean, small as a jar, pressed to the pane.

Water Plants

There is a soft knock
under the sound of the rain,
he tips his hat,
and water slides from the brim.

Rav Ada Bar Mathna is departing
to the place of study
and his wife asks: What shall I do with the children?

The youngest barely knows
yet how to smile,
her eyes stretch
each moment's delight –

wider, wider!

He replies: Are the water plants in the marshes all gone?

Vertical Path

I was charmed by holy men, women hanging on with gracious teeth, children with suckers on their feet; crowds that danced precariously, drinking to forget the angle. I chose the path for spiders, guillemots and gulls, black and white apparitions with many legs and none of the expected sense of vertigo. Drawn to a meaningful life, I infused each step with a denial of gravity.

But when I was exhausted of vertical smiles, standing 180 degrees at attention, holding so tightly to my children's hands, I fell off the path. The other way was no longer anywhere to be seen, but there was a suburban side street with buttons to select walk signals and a public school at the end of the block. Through the long hair of September music buzzed from the radio and voices filled the coffee shops.

These days I sometimes see those people from the cliff, rushing through the supermarket, clinging to the shelves, their children careful not to let up toeholds on the cart.

Buddhist Monks Don't Drive Carpool

On the radio, speakers muffled by wadded scarves, crumpled gloves, sandy slices of cheese, a spade, and a hand-rake, Buddhist monks at a temple in northeastern Ontario are being interviewed about what they do out there. Well, they don't nibble chocolate with a furrowed brow, one hand on the wheel, lunging and halting down suburban side streets. They have both hands on the wheel, out there, and a purified mind to lead them exactly nowhere.

The interview is foreshortened because the monks have a discipline not to eat after midday. It is now 11:15 and they are about to begin their last meal.

Well, it's true, I have been struggling to diet. Half-formed resolutions linger as I breathe down the final rush, brake by the school's side door.

Kids head to the van as if it were an accidental motion of their feet, hang in a group by the doorway, engage in the usual passive aggressive tactics over who sits in the back; my own children end up climbing to the rear. I'm pleased they are neither passive nor aggressive enough to win the struggle. I drop my shoulders, straighten my chin, and, inflating into my best meditative posture, head toward the horizon.

Lay-ups in a Strapless Bra

and other attempts to bring together
the things that matter most
in the twelfth year of your life
score *way too rarely*;

there is just so much that
never works out, no matter how
late you stay up with the radio on
(feeling certain the station will recognize

your loyalty through the waves),
while the lamp casts
its hoop over your sleeping crown,
steals when you least expect.

Perch

    I am
nose-touching-close
to my son's closed door,

    wind blows
through the crack at the
bottom onto my toes.

    It's January, but
he keeps his window open,
sleeps beneath a nest of blankets.

    When he was three
he put his pillow in the
freezer to make it cold.

    Always a gentle hand,
a cooling touch. His freckled grin
is loopy now with adolescence.

    He would try anything once,
brought to terror only
by the proximity of boredom,

    by having nothing
to take his mind off
his mind, just the perch before launch.

I Sleep in the Arms of Your Eyes

as my older sister slept in those sad sanctuaries
of do-not-enter, the blanket pulled over her head,
but for a downy burst of hair;

as my husband wishes sleep were a cat that crept upon him
and lay itself down without a sound,
his senses half open until morning;

as my small son sleeps in the finger-like dreams,
slipping through his breath to my face;
a trail of crumbs to return by.

Slip Through

Gone through the screen
door, into the dark
throat of November.
Leaves churn
behind my car,
the children shrug,
slow as the tide
from their beds.
I turn the ignition,
wake sound,
slip through their
thinning broadcast
of dream.

Shuttered in Traffic

The radio show this morning
is hosting a 'dream speaker'
who proceeds to gently spook
the hell out of me as I drive to work.

Dreams of teeth falling out
tell of words
that shouldn't have come
from your mouth,
matters spoken that did not belong
and now in your palm
cannot be returned.

Dreams of cotton
stuffed in your mouth
tell of words
that need a way out
but cling instead
as you mumble
and strain your tongue
to dislodge them.

In her world of strangely
perfect sense,
I wonder what she would say
of my dreams of jaws
that crack and splinter,
joints that wrench, like fault lines, apart.

What would she say when the words
once spoken, once written,
undeniable in ink and air,
break you into pieces?

Tight

The dentist's stomach
brushes the side of my face
as he works on my teeth.

I hear it rumble, turn
softly, beneath his blue scrubs.

He is the dentist I went to as a child,
still saying,

Open a little wider,
 close a little,
  take a break,
   have a rinse,
    raise a hand if there's a problem,

under his breath.
As natural as breathing.
Perhaps he says this while he sleeps.

Afterwards,
on the way home,
a 94-year-old South African woman on the radio
is speaking with the precise articulation
of her nation, each word
like the Platonic form of the word.

She tells how she spent her babyhood in
an orphanage, where there
weren't a lot of some things –
             like fruit,
                    and love.

When she says *love*
she heaves what might have been a sigh,
but turns into a sound
of unexpected,
sustained and articulate
despair.

Light snow is falling down
in slow motion,
each flake wandering up
before down.

I have a sudden urge to chase
the season's last leaves
down the street with a dustpan.

All this makes a sound in my life,
as your poems make a sound in your life –
slowly they unwind from us
and we enter new ones.

What we lose from childhood
is a perceptive style
that says, *Oh!*
   and then *oh!*
again.

The growing up of the brain
which we feed,
and water,
and rest,
and put out
in the fresh air –

purposed to inhibit the *Oh!*

So that we can
narrow our focus
and get things done.

The function of the cortex
is essentially inhibitory.

The function of poems
is essentially
to hold on.

Chords

The chords beneath my words
are all the same.

Ingested minor, relentless coughing up
of fur-covered keys,

by the cat that came back.
Her green eyes bulge,

her pupils narrow, we can only guess
about her months of survival,

but not mine. All my tribulations
tremble here.

I sit on the steps, admire
the hosta's ancient grip of clay,

the way, this year, the perennial bed
filled on its own –

a squirrel wheeling overhead;
someone's nest is full of strangers,

but not mine. The same chords
repeat, a cycle of melodic mistakes

and harmonic repair.
The same song of freckles

across a smile, a dock that
drums the waves.

Dreaming Dingo

The dog that looks
like a pincushion
sitting on a pincushion
outside Starbucks
is patiently deranged by
sub-zero winds.
Trembling into pieces.

While the quaking fur
and liquid eyes
have been bred
for appeal,
I wonder if he dreams of dingos –

flashing across
the frozen dunes of the plaza lot
dodging beach-brown Fords and Corollas,

freedom whistling through
his narrow ears and slip-thin eyes.

I once read an essay
by Barbara Kingsolver
in which she surmised
that chickens raised in a box
must think:

Well now, life is a box –
the same as they'd think
if they lived in a yard
with a fence glinting
sunlight at dawn
and blooming lupines
by afternoon:
Well now, life is a garden.

And so, perhaps, it is with this dog.

His marble gaze wavers
between dingos and anticipation:
Now he dreams of the armpit
of a down coat.

My Disbelief

is a thermal crack in
the path; something to
skirt

and step around,
looking over
shoulder, under
elbow,
down the thin abyss.

Patient company,
my disbelief is
a light tabby,
the cautious flow
of her green eyes;

or, something that bends
toward the doorway,
like sunlight's
passive vigilance.

It brings me
to the park at dusk
in the summer
to watch shade
stretch across children,

hear their voices
echo after
striking brick.

You Take a Chisel

camping
and fill your pockets
with rocks,
quartz branches,
driftwood pictures
of wind and
the brink of disaster.

Home again
you arrange them
on shelves in the garage,
on counters and trays
by your bed ,
and on the table,
like so many anchors

hinging you to
survival, to the past,
to all the collected
beauty our life
casts on, and
time casts off.

Flooding

My thoughts are flooding footprints, impossible to trace.
It's no wonder we never meet at the same place –
　　　I'm waiting in

the beating wings of a tent beneath trees on the grey shore
of Long Beach. That was a long time ago. You're tired

of this marriage that dissolves, then reassembles,
like a dream we keep having, night after night.

The Purpose of Laundry

Spilt winter
has not been
cleaning up well
this year, now that
I've learned what
happiness is:
a muscle hard to find,
somewhere in the core.

But then again,
a little mess of cold
should be nothing
to cry over.

I watch the kids
watch to see
what I will do next.

The dryer is drying its eyes,
my daughter's feet
are rubbing the wall
as she lies on her stomach
watching TV.

Sadness is what keeps house
when the other feelings
find new friends
with more beauty, and time,
and most importantly
know how to relax –

without that feeling
of losing it
whenever the work is done;

In the end,
laundry gives a person
something to do,
filling the ears with
a silencing swing.

Braced

I stare at the
icy roof,
licked white
against the robin's
egg-blue
crack of sky,
then brace again,
for our angry words,
our sharp hearts.

Spinning

An island off my dream
is drifting.

Someone in an apron
is serving food.

Someone's small son
is sleeping on the sofa.

Someone's wife is spinning
in the washer

around the walls.

Let's Say

I love you.

Or, it hurts hating you;

somewhere in
this honeycombed
night you are
sitting like a bee
as the hours
turn.

Wishing I wished
you would come
upstairs, I wish you
wouldn't.

So stay on
your couch,
you're a musical note
with the muscle
tone of a score.

Love you, *don't*.
Love you, *don't*.

The trees talk,
but in the suburbs
it's hard to hear,

heart to ear.
Stop signs
more plentiful

than flowers,
planes across the sky,
white on white.

I can't hear the next step,
yet I feel it scrape.

Marriage Review

Aromas of nicotine layered with toasted hair, cold finger tips, herbal trails and a questioning core; dry palate, melody of green tea, foggy persistence. Altogether a weedy flavour, weighty darkness and lingering, blurred finish.

Pair with children, savoury word choices of a twelve-year-old, salty wit of a nine-year-old and the heady scent of independence, open doors, less than flattering appraisal of three young adults.

Move over, Bordeaux,
melon spears, soft cheese, fig crostini.

Opening a Chamber

of his heart, he shovels something in
that will at least burn –

childhood furniture,
desk top, book end.

Something drier than all his love –
a deluge down the hatch.

No hands to pass it back now.
No one to whisper to.

Just bedrooms getting cleaner,
and the courage of tidying up.

The need to toss in something daily now –

chair frame, hamper, board game;

the engine beats with industry,
forcing nights down the track,

dawn birds nattering.
Heave it in and watch,
all of it without me.

Stretch Out

I have locked the front door,
I have locked the back door,
still you slip through.

You used to be the one
to lock up,
to stay up late,
to stay away.

Don't think I don't miss you.
That doesn't mean
we know what that means.

I stretch out, fill the sheets
you used to fill,
the dreams come so thin.

No hefty arguments to pin them down.
No hunger, anger, wish.

One Night

I make my bed with sheets from the dryer as warm as your skin. The smell of heated cotton sharp against the frigid air. This helps for one night.

The cicadas are sawing the dark into dreams; as of yet, it isn't better. You break going in, you break going out. So what if you keep a picture of me in the closet?

Eventually, the rain pelts even cicadas into silence.

Folded

Memory
precipitates
cold rain
into a season
of snow pants,
clear umbrellas
folded, no more
dripping print of
cats and dogs;
ageing is one step
forward, one step
back, a dance toward
the next embrace,
round and round
the four-wheeled
world of winter-
time again.

Words and Wind

I feel the cinch
of existence.

A paddle stroke
stirs the lake,

just eddies inside eddies,

and footsteps
in snow and leaves –

no more than
words and wind

travelling through
the trees.

It all comes together
in my mind:

cold hands,
cold nose,

banging mud, frozen
off our soles.

Mirror Neurons

Olive leaves of the mind,
silver in wind,
flicker like stars,
synapse across the skies.
Cortex, lyric,
film from the pen, from the eyes.
From one to another,
crossfire catches us all.

Notes

"Horse or No Horse" is for Lawrence and Gerry Diamond
"Brought Back" is for Laurence Hutchman
"Runaway" is for Mick Burrs

Acknowledgements

I would like to thank the editors of the publications in which the following poems originally appeared, some in earlier versions:

Cordite Poetry Review: "Marriage Review," originally published as "Marriage Review: Mine"
Echolation: "Down the Line"
Heart Anthology: "Opening a Chamber"
Letters and Pictures from the Old Suitcase: "Horse or No Horse"
Poet to Poet Anthology: "Runaway"
Red Earth Review: "Stretch Out"

Sincere thanks to the publishers of Guernica Editions, Connie McParland and Michael Mirolla, and to my dedicated and compassionate editor, Elana Wolff.

About the Author

Beverly Ellenbogen is a school psychologist whose work has appeared in several journals and anthologies, including *Saranac Review and Modern Morsels: A Selection of Short Canadian Fiction and Poetry*. She is also the author of a previous collection of poetry with Guernica Editions, *Footsteps on the Ceiling*. Beverly enthusiastically divides her time amongst many activities and interests both professional and recreational in a way that suggests she either doesn't understand the nature of time, or thinks she is more than one person. Nevertheless, she gamely thrives in a world of neuroscience, urban lakes at dawn, behaviour analysis, tiny figures made of polymer clay and the unstoppable momentum of parenting.

MIX
Paper from
responsible sources
FSC® C100212
www.fsc.org

Printed in June 2018
by Gauvin Press,
Gatineau, Québec